YOUNG ENGINEERS

Building Structures and Towers

by Tammy Enz

raintree

a Capstone company — publishers for children

Raintree is an imprint of Capstone Global Library Limited, a company incorporated in England and Wales having its registered office at 264 Banbury Road, Oxford OX2 7DY – Registered company number: 6695582

www.raintree.co.uk
myorders@raintree.co.uk

Edited by Adrian Vigliano
Designed by Philippa Jenkins
Picture research by Svetlana Zhurkin
Production by Katy LaVigne
Originated by Capstone Global Library Ltd
Printed and bound in India.

ISBN 978 1 4747 3704 3 (hardback)
21 20 19 18 17
10 9 8 7 6 5 4 3 2 1

ISBN 978 1 4747 3708 1 (paperback)
21 20 19 18 17
10 9 8 7 6 5 4 3 2 1

British Library Cataloguing in Publication Data
A full catalogue record for this book is available from the British Library.

Acknowledgements
We would like to thank the following for permission to reproduce photographs:
Capstone Studio: Karon Dubke, cover, 8, 9, 12, 13, 16, 17, 20, 21, 24, 25, 26, 27; Shutterstock: Aha-Soft, 7, Darryl Brooks, 5, Olga Morozova, 23, pedrosala, 19, rootstock, 11, topnatthapon, 15, VOJTa Herout, 29
We would like to thank Harold Pratt for his help in the preparation of this book.

Every effort has been made to contact copyright holders of material reproduced in this book. Any omissions will be rectified in subsequent printings if notice is given to the publisher.

All the internet addresses (URLs) given in this book were valid at the time of going to press. However, due to the dynamic nature of the internet, some addresses may have changed, or sites may have changed or ceased to exist since publication. While the author and publisher regret any inconvenience this may cause readers, no responsibility for any such changes can be accepted by either the author or the publisher.

Contents

Some words are shown in bold, **like this.** You can find out what they mean by looking in the glossary.

What is a structure?

Structures are all around us. Most people live in a structure. You pass lots of them when you go out. Structures and towers can be almost any size or shape. But they are built from many of the same parts. These important parts may be hidden under ground, beneath floors or inside walls. But they are the keys to holding up buildings and keeping you safe.

What kinds of structures do you see every day?

Footings and foundations

The first step in building a structure is making a **foundation**. Without foundations, heavy buildings would sink into the soft soil beneath them. Sometimes structures sit on buried concrete columns called **piers**. Piers carry a building's weight to sturdy rock layers beneath the soil. Other structures sit on **footings**. These large slabs of concrete spread out a building's weight.

piers

Piers are designed to support a structure's full weight.

Experiment with footings

See how footings work in
this experiment.

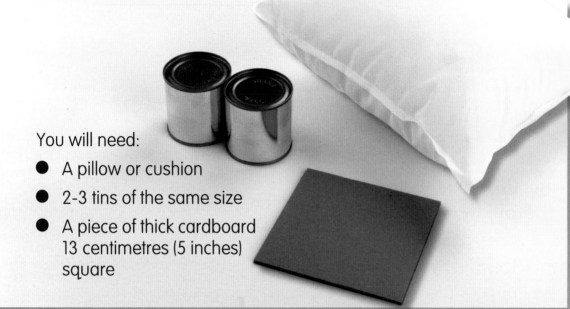

You will need:
- A pillow or cushion
- 2-3 tins of the same size
- A piece of thick cardboard
  13 centimetres (5 inches)
  square

1. Place the
   pillow on the
   floor. Set
   a tin on its
   centre.

2. Stack another tin on top. What happens?

3. Remove the tins and lay the cardboard on the pillow.

4. Stack tins on the cardboard. What happens now? Do the tins sink in as far? Are they more stable?

Beams and joists

Beams and **joists** are the structural parts of floors and roofs. They are often hidden beneath floors or above ceilings. Beams need to be strong enough to support people and things stored in buildings. Beams come in different shapes and sizes. They can be made from wood, steel or concrete. Joists are the horizontal pieces that support a floor or ceiling. Joists are made from small pieces of steel or wood connected together.

joists

Beams and joists form the strong skeleton of a structure.

11

Experiment with beams

Beams are placed on their edges, not on their flat faces. This allows them to carry more weight. See how it works with this experiment.

You will need:

- 2 empty cereal boxes
- Tape
- 2 stacks of books
- 2-3 tins of equal size

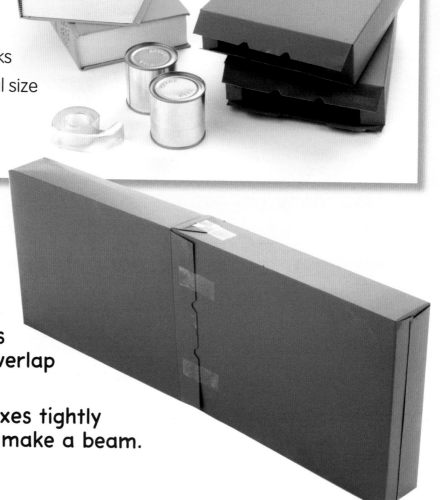

1. Place the open ends of the boxes together. Overlap their tabs.

2. Tape the boxes tightly together to make a beam.

3. Place the beam on its edge spanning the book stacks.
4. Place tins on the middle of the beam. How many tins can it hold?

5. Now place the beam on its face spanning the books.
6. How many tins can it hold now?

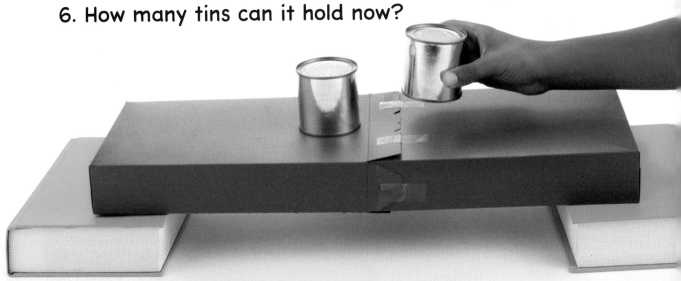

When loaded, beams experience **tension** and **compression** forces. Tension forces stretch parts of beams. Compression forces squash other parts. Beams that are too compressed **buckle.** Beams that have too much tension tend to snap. Steel and wooded beams stay strong when stretched and squashed. But concrete beams need to be reinforced to stay strong.

compression

tension

Engineers must carefully balance forces in their building designs.

15

Modeling a reinforced concrete beam

Concrete beams break easily. But with a little help from steel **reinforcing** bars they remain strong. Make your own reinforced beam.

You will need:

- Pieces of polystyrene foam about 5 cm (2 in) x 13 cm (5 in) x 3 cm (1 in) thick
- 2 wooden skewers

1. Hold the ends of the foam and slowly bend it until its bottom begins to crack.

2. Carefully slide the skewers into the foam about 1 cm (¼ in) from the bottom of the beam. Place them about 3 cm (1 in) apart.

3. Now bend the beam again. Do the skewers keep the beam strong?

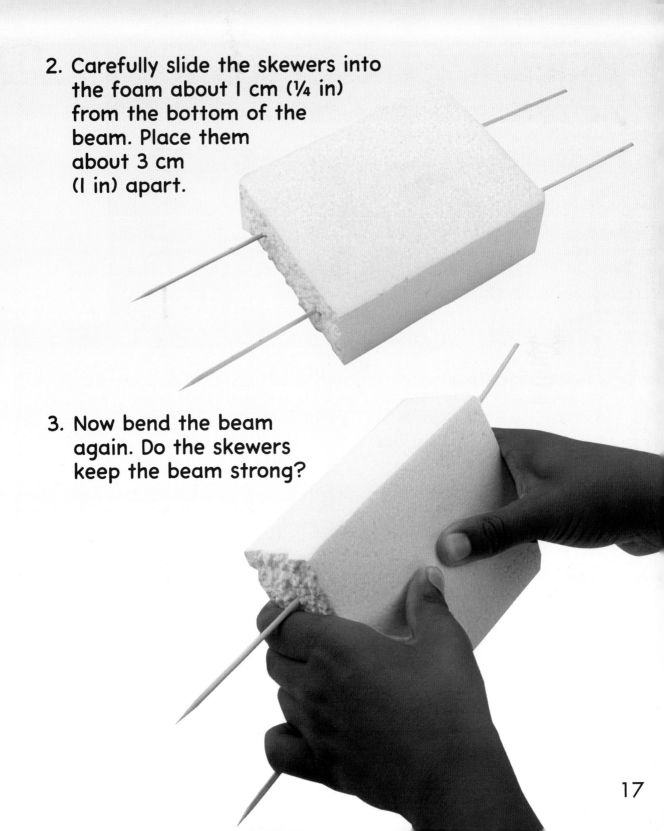

Columns

Beams support all the weight of the things inside a building. But **columns** support that weight and the weight of the building itself and carry all of it to the foundation. Beams at each building level connect to columns. Columns can be any shape, but often have square or circle **cross sections**. Longer columns are less stable than shorter columns and buckle more easily when loaded.

Columns help engineers to create buildings with many floors.

columns

19

Experiment with columns

Test out the strength of long and short columns with this experiment.

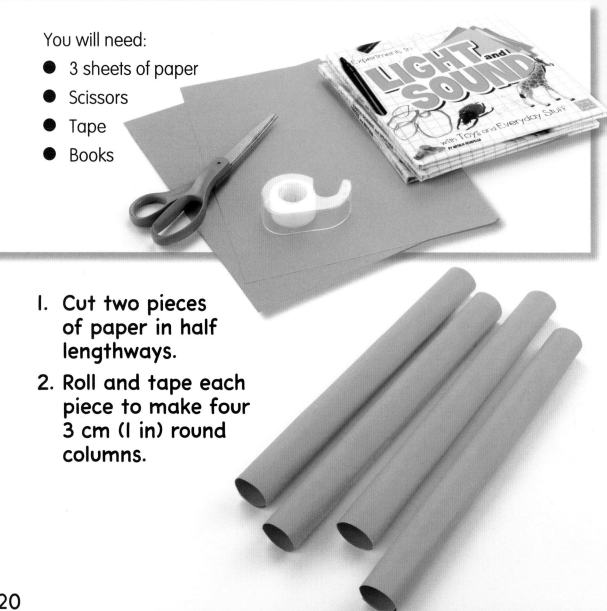

You will need:

- 3 sheets of paper
- Scissors
- Tape
- Books

1. Cut two pieces of paper in half lengthways.

2. Roll and tape each piece to make four 3 cm (1 in) round columns.

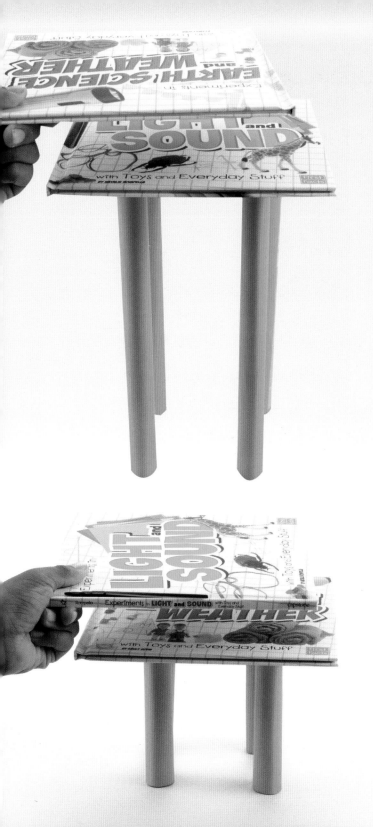

3. Place a column under each corner of a book. Carefully stack on more books, one at a time. How many books can the long columns hold?

4. Cut another paper into quarters. Roll and tape each of these pieces to make four short columns.

5. Load up the short columns with books. Can they hold more?

X-braces and shear walls

Beams and columns support lots of weight. But there's more to making a building or tower stand straight and tall. A **lateral,** or sideways, system prevents wind from toppling structures. **X-braces** and **shear walls** collect wind forces and carry them to the foundation. You may not see these braces but even tall glass buildings have hidden lateral systems.

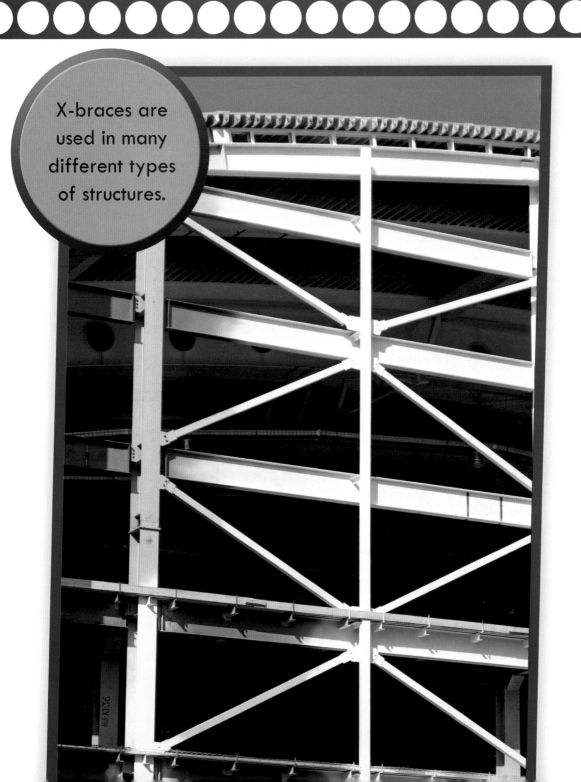

X-braces are used in many different types of structures.

23

Experiment with shear walls

Shear walls are walls inside buildings that carry wind loads to the foundation. See how they work with this experiment.

You will need:

- Empty cereal box
- Tape

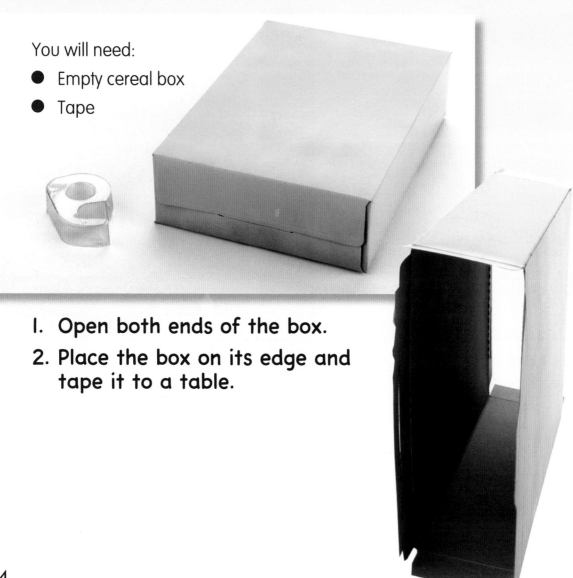

1. Open both ends of the box.
2. Place the box on its edge and tape it to a table.

3. Push against one side of the box. How easily does the box tilt?

4. Now tape the open ends of the box closed to create shear walls.

5. Push against the side as before. What happens now? Do the shear walls prevent tilting?

Build a braced tower

X-bracing is another way to keep buildings straight and tall when wind blows on them. See how it works with this experiment.

You will need:

- Spaghetti noodles
- American hard gums

1. Break two noodles in half. Use hard gums to connect the pieces into a square.
2. Repeat step 1 to make another square.

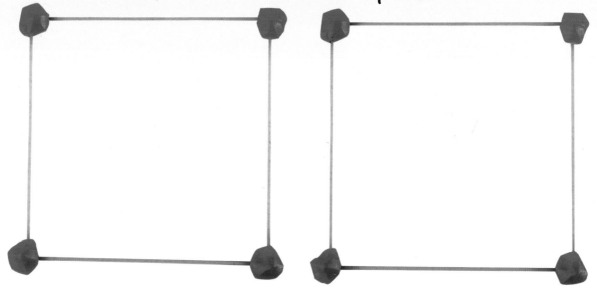

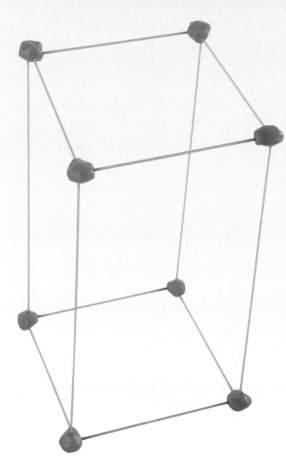

3. Break a 3 cm (1 in) piece off four more noodles.

4. Use these long noodles as columns to connect the squares into a tower.

5. Push sideways on the top of the tower. What happens?

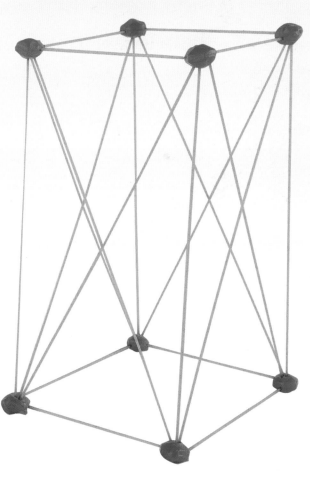

6. Add noodle x's across each side of the tower. Now what happens when you push sideways?

Structures and towers are amazing to look at. But there's more to them than meets the eye. You know about their important parts. They all need foundations. They also need beams and columns to carry the weight of people and objects inside them. Just as important are braces and walls to keep them tall and straight when the wind blows.

Engineers work hard each day to design the next great building.

Glossary

beam support for floors and roofs

buckle to bend under force

column upright support pillar

compression force that squashes

cross section shape you see when you cut through something

footing wide concrete slab under a building column

foundation support at the bottom of a building

joist beam made from short pieces of steel or wood supporting part of the structure of a building; horizontal piece that supports a floor or ceiling

lateral sideways

pier underground support column

reinforcing making stronger

shear wall wall designed to resist wind forces

structure load carrying parts of a building

tension pulling force

X-brace crossing members that resist wind forces

Find out more

Books

Man-Made Wonders (Worldwide Wonders),
 (Wayland, 2016)
Record-Breaking Buildings (Infographic Top 10),
 Jon Richards and Ed Simkins (Wayland, 2016)
Super Cool Construction Activities with Max Axiom
 (Max Axiom Science and Engineering Activities),
 Tammy Enz (Raintree, 2015)

Websites

www.bbc.co.uk/guides/zqyr9j6
Find out how skyscrapers are built on the BBC
iWonder site.

www.funkidslive.com/learn/building-london
Discover all the different types of buildings you can
find across the city of London.

Index